Following In His Footsteps

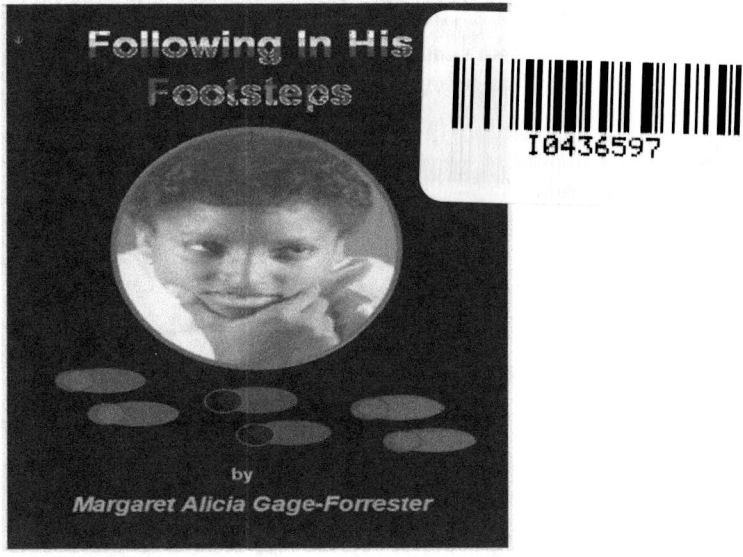

Was first written and published

by.

M. A. Gage-Forrester

London

07958122727

Paypal https://www.paypal.me/MAliciaGageForrester

Email margaret69523@yahoo.com

Typeset by and illustrated by
Margaret Alicia Gage-Forrester

All Rights Reserved

Commission...

"Whatever your hands find to do, do it!..."

"Following In His Footsteps" is a spring off from my spiritual encounter with God through his word and deep meditation. I, Margaret Alicia Gage-Forrester produced this booklet of poetry which is a compilation of stories over the years as the Holy Spirit inspired me. As a generation of my grandfather Thomas Joseph Gage, known as TG an established poet and writer and my mother Mary Sonia (Gage) (Farrell) Cabey, his only daughter from which my bloodline seem to have inherited the same trend of writing and articulation in poetic artform expressively in different genres.

I, Margaret Alicia Gage-Forrester sit down to contemplate things, often my thoughts run into poetry and hook lines of songs, and surmonettes, etc. I guess writing is dug deep in the veins, hence formulating and gesticulating poetry just happens.

I am the eldest of six (6) children of My mother Mary Sonia (Gage)(Farrell) Cabey, the only child of grandfather of T. J. Gage.

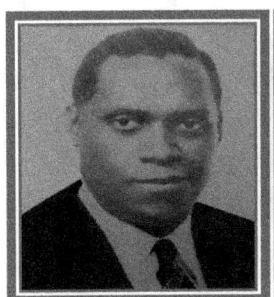 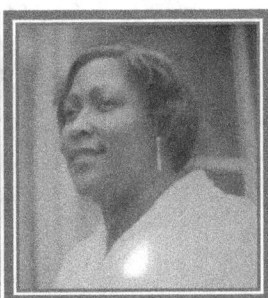 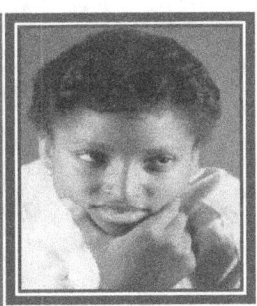

To be fair, all six children expresses themselves in a variety of creative art forms: poetry, singing, rapping, stand-up comedy, graphic designing, drawing with brush and paint, music creation. I acknowledge and honour all my generation's artistry, especially, grandfather, T. J. Gage known as TG whom they recorded to have died at eighty-seven (87) years old in 2016, my Mother M. Sonia (Gage)(Farrell)Cabey who died at fifty (50) years old in 2003 and my father Phillip George Forrester a musician who was also recorded as dead in my absence in June 26th, 2014.

I demonstrate the same recognisable talent that has feed down through the generations in my work. I, Margaret Alicia Gage-Forrester, am a Christian, loving God, other people and myself too, so most of my writings are biblically based, inspired by the Holy Spirit to capture the audience.

This book is an amalgamation of poetic writing by the generations, namely Wilston JORDAIN (OutlawTheArtist) Rueben Johnson (my son, 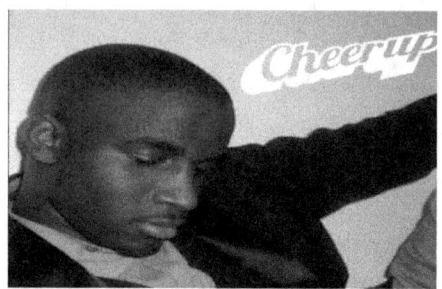 grandson and great grandson to Sonia (Gage)(Farrell)Cabey and Thomas Joseph Gage, my generations of writers and announciators. Jordain Johnson is a poet, lyricist, rapping artist and spoken word artist in his own right which was recognised from a young age. Grandfather's writings are also in this book.

My brothers and sister have contributed to this book with their artistry, namely: Joseph (ScribeTheVerbalist) Javayne Cabey, Zachary (Nimbe) Kenrick Cabey and Christelle N. Cabey, but writings are mainly by myself, Margaret Alicia (Elisha)(carried Farrell, Cabey) Gage-Forrester.

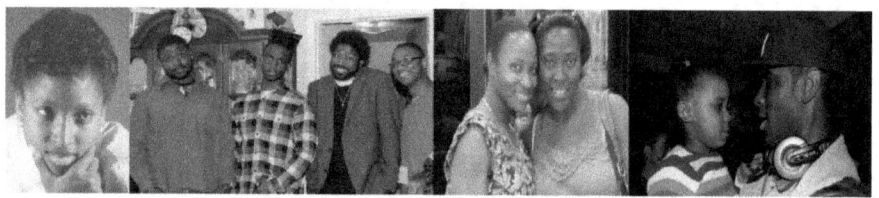

Poetry speaks repeatedly even when words and the poets themselves are no more. So hope you can journey with me through circumstance, scenery and time in this book of poems called, **"Following In His Footsteps"**.

By Margaret Alicia (AnnaMoriah, Elisha) Gage-Forrester

Content Page

Those Hands

Those hands hidden in your jacket

Use them for right and they'll put money in your pocket,

Reflect on the attention your mothers put on those hands,

A good review bound to propel you to advance,

Those hands were made for something special,

Don't sit there and be in denial,

Take up the pencil, take up the pen,

Ask for the slate, ask for the paper, then

Sit down and use them,

Those hands, envision those hands,

How many times before, you heard commands,

Your hands are connected to your brain, your eyes, your ear,

Portray what you understand, see and hear and don't shed a tear.

by

Margaret Alicia Gage-Forrester

Acknowledge Them Both

We value our mothers, we value our fathers,
No, there is no one sided story, they both were in the matter,
Praise one, deliberately leave out the other,
No! Will we always set out to conjecture,
Some didn't have the right method,
Their expressions came with a thud,
However, did you realize, it is a new year,
Let's all affirmatively begin to repair,
We remember the effects of our grandfathers,
We pray for positive actions from our fathers,
Determining to see them rise to another level,
With corrective measures reaching the adjoining bevel,
Many of us were raised without a father,
But yet, your qualities are not only mother but also father,
So hooray for mother
And hooray to father.

By

Margaret Alicia Gage-Forrester

God gave me a son and I am grateful for the father who never through his sperm on the ground. Onan, in the bible, died for doing such a thing for God was not pleased. I came together consentedly and a child was birth into this world. Thank you, dad, for, "Not spilling the bean".

Be fruitful and multiply and replenish the earth, was the instructions from the book, the Bible. Jesus also said, suffer the little children to come unto me and forbid them not for of such is the kingdom of heaven. Under whatever circumstances we make our children God still want to bless them.

I am thankful to God that I was apart of the equation to multiply and replenish the earth. Thank you dad for been apart of the equation too.

Thank you, Father, for allowing me to have child birth from my womb. Thank Jesus, Amen! Hallelujah!

My little friend Alfie

Well, Well, Who Could Tell,
You would never be able to tell,
Sitting at the ledge of the window.
Waiting to greet little Alfie, hello!
Jeering his words as daddy emphasize,
And listening to hear his words in surprise.
Dad says Becareful, his echo says, careful!
I reiterated from my window, yes, careful!
And little Alfie echoed again, careful!
The yellow water sprout flower open its fan,
And little Alfie picks 3, no more than,
One for mommy, One for daddy,
One for me and sometimes granny,
What colour is it, Alfie says yellow
Without a struggle he just bellows, yellow,
Piercing his eyes upward daily,
He said, Mom, I talk to the lady.
One evening My sister heard the baby,
And I do not know, maybe there is jealousy,
Because her disposition became even more lousy,
The family car changed to grey,
And Little Alfie began to cry each day,
Alfie finding no connection with grey,
Mom had to clothe Alfie with much colour each day,
Trying to find calm as they step outside in the dawn of the day,
BUT only the yellow number plate could, curb the sigh of grey.

By: Margaret Alicia Gage-Forrester

PS.

As families we have to be sensitive to our children pleasure too. Little Alfie was
having no fun without colours on a backdrop of grey.

So to compensate the unwanted grey, mommy had to introduce playful items with
much colours to appease the growing needs of the young man Alfie.

In observing little Alfie grow it appears to me we have to come up with different ways
of teaching them at elementary for their little brains are full already with words and
scenes from the children television shows and mom and dad interaction that to go
back and teach them to recognise letters is a joke, for they already know how to
string sentences fluently and interpret pictures at 2 years old.

So what do we do?

That Tree, That Big Big Tree

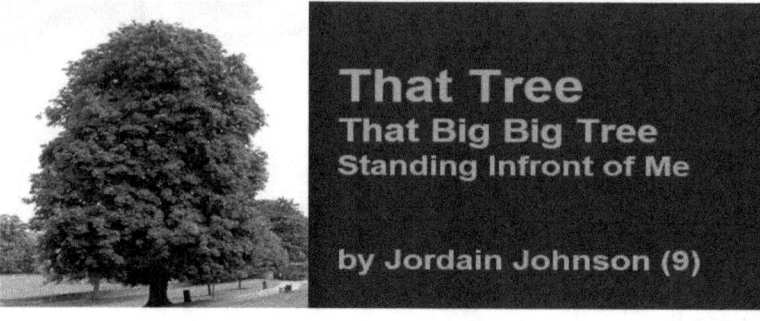

That Tree
That Big Big Tree
Standing Infront of Me

by Jordain Johnson (9)

February 17th , 2000

That tree, that big big tree,
It really annoys me,
Because it sounds like a bee,
I got to do something about that big big tree,
I'm going to die unless it dies before me,
I'm so mad at that big big tree, standing infront of me.
What can I do about that big big tree?
Cut it down, but it is too big for me,
I need to get my daddy to help me,
That Tree, That big big tree,
Why does it have to stand infront of me?

Written by my son,

Wilston Jordain (WJRJ) "OutlawTheArtist" Reuben Johnson

**New York, PS55 Primary School,
Bronx, New York, USA**

Speak Just!

Speak just, and none can call thee liar,
Speak hate, your tongue is on hire.
This tongue - deceptive in its course,
Brought low, the creator of the universe.

And if in God one's humble staid and meek
And it's commands and admonishions seek,
None can confront thee, no matter whence he came,
Should he but seek to ridicule Christ name.

Speak just, the Lord is on your side,
And no earthly power against this can abide!
Tise up Man, give the Lord His due,
Stand firm! t'was He who died for you.

Speak just, then stand and contemplate,
Thy blessings round about, though others rave and hate,
Oh that bitter day of Jesus' sweet salvation,
He fought the depths of hell for your redemption.

By

Thomas J. Gage (TG), my grandfather.

It has always being the principles of my family generational bloodline to be as truthful and honest as we can possibly be in all circumstances. We speak just!

Happy Birthday My Son 13/11/2017

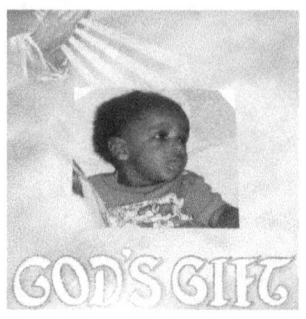

GOD'S GIFT

Jordain Johnson 26+

Son, it was years ago that you made me a mom,
Time slipped by so fast, counting 26+, Wow! says mom,
A joy to carry in my belly, a joy to carry as you grew up,
Should I have fault you, no, you did well as you develop,
Now you are a man, standing on your own ,

My God, let him practice what he learned,
The dangers of this world tossing on his life,
But God, never let him get too engulf and miss out on eternal life.
I only had one chance to raise you,
Any mistake unfortunately, I cannot undo,
So make the best of what you got,
And hold your head up high and don't stay in the rot,

Love you son!
Love you so, but the greatest love you can have,
comes from above.
May God's Holy Spirit guide you, protect you,
and rest upon you like a dove.
Seek to serve and glorify Him no matter your
endeavour,
For it is Him who wants to flow out of your belly
like a river.

HAPPY BIRTHDAY MY SON!

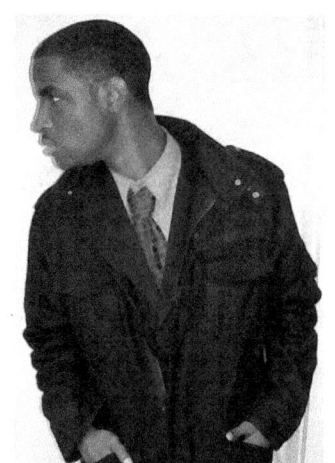

And like today 13th November May you count
many many more,
Not in pain or sorrow but with prosperity in
abundance and a bright hope for tomorrow.

God Jehovah Yahweh Bless you my son in Jesus name, through the aid of the
Holy Spirit, Amen! Alleluia

from your mother

13 November, 2017 1 11am GMT

I am thankful to God for this opportunity to be your mom, Hallelujah!

Every Good Deed I DO I Do For God

Every good deed I do, I do for God.
Every bad deed I do, drives me beneath the sod
Oh, how I'm torn apart by strife,
And yet I know that I must love my life,
To please my God.

Every good thing I say,
Makes me feel good.
Every bad thing I say in degradation emerges rude.
In deep regret and sombre attitude
I rise bewildered, wishing that the day
Would curb my tongue of foolish platitude.

Everyone I love, my love is quite sincere,
And they who do not care for me,
For them, I shouldn't care;
Yet this is wrong and goes against the grain,
And make good things a burden and strain.

by my grandfather

Thomas Joseph Gage

THE CHRIST CHILD

All have sinned and come short of the glory of God,
So the Father sent his only begotten son, our saviour and Lord,
Born of a virgin, with redemptive power within,
Shepherds follow the star which led them to his lodging,
They brought gifts of frankincense, gold and myrrh,
And was instructed, travel not back the same way anymore.

From an infant, they pursued the Christ child,
But God the father sent angels to be his guide,
He lived among the people with outstanding wisdom,
Until his time of commission was come,
The Christ child bore pain and suffering,
Sacrifice that would leave others shuddering.

He died and rose again,
Giving hope to all his children,
His work on earth was finished,
And new life he has furnished,
So while we celebrate this his birth,
May we never forget his worth.

The Christ child
For God so loved the world he gave his only begotten Son,
That whosoever believeth in him will not perish but have
eternal life.

by Alicia Gage-Forrester 2023

Teach Me

O God of heaven and earth
If thou art for me
Then guide me in
To stay in tune with thee

Hide not thy face at anytime
Give me the courage bold
Bless me with thy love subline
Give me thy hand to hold

Teach me to honour thy works
Teach me to love you more
Teach me that nothing ever mocks
The glory of thy shore

By Thomas J Gage

<u>This Jesus</u>

Believe me souls, God heart is glad

For you and I've thriven

To reach out from a world so sad

And grasped this Jesus given

Yes this love his only son

Not in this world another

He gave his everlasting one

And chose to call me brother

It's not enough to bow my head

Or go down on my knees

For everything in me was dead

Till Jesus came for me

By Thomas J Gage

How Many Times

How many times had Jesus stood
And listened while you prayed
How many answers hath he given
And yet your spirit strayed
How many times you called aloud
Then wandered from the spot
Then Jesus, drawing in a cloud
Found that you were not
And yet he stands there, waiting still
With heart and hands so free
He never tires, never will
His blood's on Calvary
He cannot turn, He came to save
Through bitter, bitter strife
A sinner who was lost
He ransomed with his life

by my grandfather

Thomas Joseph Gage

Grateful! O So Grateful!

Grateful for the times you cared outside yourself,
For the many tears you shed when;
Asking God, Please improve the steps of my children,
For the times you toiled long hard years over people's stuff,
Ironing, cleaning, yes, in service you done it all, though it was rough, tough,
For times you spent imparting knowledge, manners and behaviour,
We've heard them all and we'll keep them forever.

Grateful for the turbulent tumultuous winds you bare,
While been bashed about in your career,
For the countless hammering you took,
In this ever-changing world that kept you in the book,
If there was a moment to share,
Could we, would we be able to compare?
We knew you were out there,
But did we even show that we care, so unfair,
But this, I want to let you know, I care,
I am grateful, O, so grateful.

Grateful you fought in the wars for England,
You may not have gotten the praises deserved,
Still you had to fight again in civil conflicts, just to be housed,
And for a decent standard of living in this land.
True, some went off the rail
Breaking the very things you fought to maintain and to hail,
But don't despair, still believe...
We will continue to achieve...
Yes, to improve your name,
Your game, and even your fame.

There were five and ten in a crowded flat, no room to spare,
Some worked night, some worked day, just so the space could share,
Set out shivering at twilight, through the deep freezing snow,
Get there, long roads to trod, but no one wants to know,
Covering with crumpled newspaper for warmth,
Start in the dark, if you must, but miss, you can't,
Grateful for the bravery you put up,
Knowing how you conquered, we will keep our chin up,
I am grateful, O so grateful.

Today we are shining, we shine,
No, you didn't waste your time, We are becoming
Politicians, lawyers, doctors, educators, preachers, yes, we are gaining
World class and Olympic champions, and record holders in racing.

Your struggles were not in vain nor gone unnoticed,
As we progress, we are putting things into practice,
We won't throw dust in your faces,
No! We are indeed running the races,
Towards the finish line we go, purposeful,
To you and for you, our hearts forever grateful.
Grateful! Grateful! O, so grateful.

By

Margaret Alicia (Farrell) (Cabey) Gage-Forrester

In memory of the elderly people I ministered to every other Sunday in Peppie Close, Stoke Newington, London, United Kingdom in some ministerial capacity 2002-2013

Thank God also for my brothers and fathers who toiled long hard years in difficult situations in service to others. Amen!

I am also thankful for the opportunity to minister to elderly people in Montserrat through the Catholic outreach ministry program in 2016-2017.

Thank God for my sisters and mothers who invested in the children. Amen! God bless you all!

To the many who toiled long and hard years for the welfare of our people and countries, we say, **"Your work have not gone unnoticed, we are grateful!"**

Grateful!

from

Margaret Alicia Gage-Forrester

I Am Satisfied

I am Satisfied in control and in reason
with what The Lord Jehovah, Yahweh has allocated to me,
For I know the Lord is the best,
 And he gives good gifts to his children.
I am satisfied, His gifts are justified,
Hence I have no reason to be unsatisfied,
So I will press on towards the future,
For I know the Lord make no mistake we can conjecture,
Hence I am satisfied,
Through him I am justified,
So I have no reason to be unsatisfied,
I am resolutely satisfied,
Amen!

by

Margaret Alicia Gage-Forrester

"I am satisfied in control and in reason"
These are words I got while in a deep time of warfare prayer with the Lord.
I heard people repeating it saying they are done with their old ways they have now become satisfied in control and in reason.

They going back to their husband, going back to their wife,
They are going to stop all the bad things they were doing for they have become SATISFIED that God's allocation is enough to satisfy them, etc. Amen!

It was like a testimony and confession call-in show and I was the moderator mediating between the old and the new, breaking off strongholds in the name of Jesus.

I saw the people who they were attached to and I heard the names. I had to be in spiritual warfare praying hundreds of people out of the old situation telling them their husband waiting or their wife waiting etc. The prayers originally were to release one person from all these attachments. Sexual sin of Adultery, Fornication, Homosexuality, Lesbianism, etc. This was an overwhelming experience that actually happened in 2013. Spiritual warfare.

Paul was not a nice person under the name Saul for he persecuted the Church of Christ Believers but God transformed him and used him to reach the same people he was afflicting. The same thing that was your weakness, God can clean you up and use it as a strength in your life to help others. Praise God!

I am no saint save Jesus. But I heard one minister say, "The venom becomes the serum". So true. I, Margaret Alicia Gage-Forrester, says, where there is no venom if you keep putting serum, the serum can becomes the venom and then you fight with the same serum to cure the venom you attached to the body. Yes, the serum can become the cure for venom you introduce. Becareful with the urgency to add serum for precautionary measures and as observative measures for you might be giving people diseases and not curing them. Paul was cured and in much tribulation was sent on a mission with his bucket of experience to heal others of their folly.

If we confess our sins, he is faithful and just to forgive us our sins and to cleanse us from all unrighteousness. 1 John 1:19. God can take you from an over excessive cleaving into one of satisfaction. I am satisfied in control, and in reason.

*Become satisfied in God and let him use your shortcomings as cure for others, Amen! "...**His strength is made perfect in weakness...**"*
2 Corinthians 12 9

*Nothing fancy about the words, **"I am satisfied in control and in reason"**, those are the words God used with some anointed prayers. Yes, God desire to restore our life and to get us in a prepared state for when he returns. Become satisfied in Him. Amen! God bless you all!*

Holding Rope Down A Slippery Slope

The cares of life, did sleep,
Mansion high, you imagine, so deep,
Set your eyes on the gold,
That Jesus Christ will hold,
Consider the fact that you are not alone,
Tribulation mounting, but sin, hope never to condone.

Jehovah God knows this is no joke,
Under confines which daily provoke,
Piercing eyes look for hope,
Some go outside to take in dope,
Others try to constrain on the slippery slope,
Thinking hopefully there is a holding rope.

You cannot tell from day to day,
When your character will be mark down the way.
Sunset to sundown we sit and wait,
To hear the plight of our estate.
So talk with Sally and Ann, is it play?
Or an opportunity to say you are acting gay.

Lord help this little child to convey,
A canvas full of contentment and not dismay,
Knowing you are the only everlasting hope for today,
Go before and Follow me Lord, for my way did sway,
Having to contemplate on the wrongs of the day
I sit, recognising, without hope in God, there isn't much to say.

By
Margaret Alicia (Farrell) (Cabey) Gage-Forrester

Design To Banish Hate

Can you with me for just one moment,
Pause to contemplate,
The wonders of this statement,
Designed to banish hate.

For God so loved the world,
He gave his only begotten son,
That whosoever believeth in him,
Will not perish but have eternal life.

By grandfather

Thomas Joseph Gage (TG)

Simple but profound words that a familiar to all from John 3 16. The God of Love invites us in, the whosoevers. Are you a whosoever today? If you have not believed yet I invite you to do so today, the access is open to anyone who would believe, the Whosoevers.

Father, Jehovah, Yahweh, God Almighty, the I Am,

I love you. Forgive me Lord, come into my heart and save me through your son shed blood. Wash me clean from sin and make me more like you. I want to be ready when you return Jesus, so please Father lead me by your Holy Spirit, teach me, cover me, direct me, deliver me into your righteousness, so I will NOT return to sin. Let sin not have dominion over me in Jesus name through the aid of the Holy Spirit.

Thank you Father for delivering me through the Holy Spirit wooing in the name Jesus Christ, Amen Alleluia! I am a new creation in Christ Jesus.

Don't Quit!

Don't quit, don't quit!
Don't quit, don't quit!
We cannot quit, no we must not quit!
What a waste that would be if we quit.

Sometimes we bend down low,
But we get up strong.

Don't quit, don't quit
Don't quit, don't quit,
We cannot quit,
No, we must not quit,
What a waste that would be if we quit.

By Margaret Alicia Gage-Forrester

This is a song

I keep Pressing,   I press towards the mark of the prize

of the high calling of God in Christ Jesus. **Philippians 3 14**

Greenness Can't Done

Screaming beams of light shine through,
No shortage of Vitamin B12 in view,
Can you imagine streams of sweat flooding the pores,
As you walk bravely in the sunshine outdoors?
Dry season wants reminder of what was done,
But a little rain on God's earth spreads greenness can't done.
The controller of seasons and time has won,
As the lush green vegetation contagiously run,
It leaves no trail of dullness,
The Emerald green attracts only brightness,

Caribbean you will see greenness again,
Please don't crumble and bend,
The world is in **turmoil** together,
Hand in hand we will recover.

by

Margaret Alicia Gage-Forrester

There is hope that we will recover, even the vegetation telling us a story.
Greenness reappear, greenness can't done.

My Dominican brother said, We will rise!
My son, "OutlawTheArtist" refers to, No blacked out disguise ...But that
we should be sticking together through Hurricane and any weather.
I say, This is your moment, this is your hour.
Shine resilient people, we've got divine favour .

We will rise! Life will flourish again in you...

Keep positivity flowing in whatever you do.

It is not over until God says it is over,
So watch and pray while the nation recover.

So Close, Yet He slighted

God has no match,
Angels and mortals must have known this,
So what prompted Lucifer, his thought to aspire,
This high angel, once the universal fire,
Becomes forever, the everlasting looser,
He was so close to God, yet he slighted
Could one have been, better knighted?
Craving the ambitions to rise above God,
Seeking followers and them who will call him Lord,
But Michael the archangel conquered Lucifer, the dragon,
Satan, that old serpent, who is now eternally barred from heaven,
He is now breaking forth with sinful traps as an eternal leaven

Excerpt from God Has No Match
By Thomas Joseph Gage

By

Margaret Alicia Gage-Forrester

"A little leaven leaveneth the whole lump"

Stop That Bullying, Chillaxilate!

Tell them stop that Bull! Yes, stop that bullying!
Stop trying to take over the world with their overpowering intimidating
spirit,
The world is huge, we all have space to share on the earth within it,
It is not right, that people would work so hard,
To destroy what our mothers and fathers fight long and hard,
Through much pain, to maintain and to hail,
As they in their badself, go off the rail.
Pull us back on track to exhibit manners and behaviour,
Not only pass down by our superiors but because we pursue right, our
Saviour.

Life is one big chocolate milkshake,
Shake it well and we are bound to have less mistakes,
The shake will give us less headaches and keep us awake,
Fresh invigoration keeps our minds until daybreak,
So take, Take and study the content of the milkshake.
Come on this journey with me to create,
Moves, that draw you closer to chillaxilate,
The internet is our oyster, let us make it great,
Instead of pulsating on things not good to meditate.

So Yes, stop that bull! Stop that bullying,
Chillaxilate and wait at the gate,
Make no negative advances to h8te,
Stop evil advances and try to positively relate,
As you inwardly correlate wait for your chance to recuperate,
With implicit intelligent, explicitly swift to demonstrate,
In a world where bad energy wants to dominate.

So Yes, let us stop that bull!
Stop that bullying.

By
Margaret Alicia Gage-Forrester
They that wait upon the Lord: 1. he shall renew their strength; 2. they
shall mount up with wings as eagles; 3. they shall run and not be weary;
4.they shall walk and not faint.

This poem is a springboard generated from the word bank of my son Wilston Jordain Reuben Johnson, A lyricist, rapper, songwriter etc.

CHILLAXILATE is to relax. Make fun of things rather than being so serious. To chill out.

This artwork was designed by my son when he was in college for a project he called " Stop that Bull****, Stop that bullying"

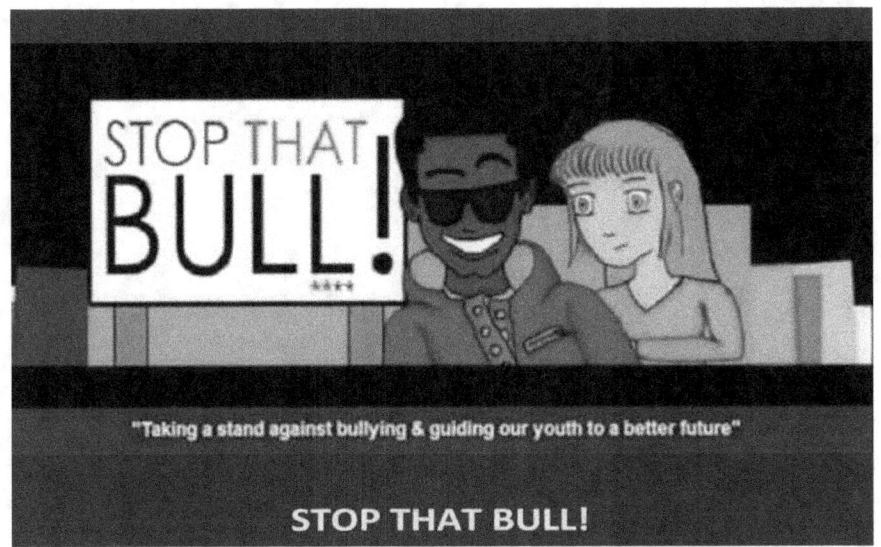

Lament To My Child
By TG 1977

Judge me not harshly child
For I was away,
Things were so different then,
I had to live that way.

When I kissed you all goodbye,
That ugly ugly morn,
Would I have gone, could I but read,
The future in that dawn.

I left you in my mother's care,
For whom else would I trust?
I couldn't stay, I had to go,
To live, to learn, I must.

Judge me not harshly child,
Life was not as today,
Montserrat had no TV set,
No Radio, night and day,

No disco-dancing, jump-up and prancing,
Respect was not a game,
And everyone looked forward to something,
Of more or less the same.

Few ships came, and few cars too,
Men looked and worked with a will,
Some plodded, went down the valley,
And some went up the hill.

Can you imagine the sign-craft art?
A wizard with brush and paint,
Depending on a government start,
To ply his trade or faint?

The first to put the stop-signs down,
The first to paint the street,
Officials of government round Plymouth town,
Pronounced my work, so neat.

At Blackbourne Airport, all the signs,
That welcomed travellers in,
And bade them advice were good designs,
Your Father worked with a will,
Your father worked, to win.

By my grandfather
Thomas Joseph Gage

Thomas Joseph Gage, my grandfather, like many West Indies people in the 1940s, 1950s and 1960s, left the West Indies in boats, heading to England and the Americas in the hope of making a better future for themselves, and to be able to send back produce for their families and even call for their families to join them sometime in the future. This worked out successfully as planned for some, but many others didn't make it.

Some of the children and families left behind did not understand, for the feeling of abandonment felt greater than the gifts, barrels and letters they would receive from time to time. They wanted the missing parent. Thomas J Gage was asking for his daughter to not judge him, because he was one who left. He sort to justify his move through the words of this poem, "Lament To My Child".

Many West Indies people can relate to this feeling and may have found solace in the poetic words, expressed by Thomas Joseph Gage (TG) since 1977.

I had an opportunity to see a lady well up with tears as I read my own poem Grateful! And she expressed the feeling of deep sadness and loss as she was not able to enjoy her father because he came to England to serve. She was also sad because she thought they were not recognized for their hard work and often people didn't understand what they went through, to be able to survive in these countries, namely America and England which they migrated to for a better life. She went on to thank me for the poem because it resignated with her and her dad struggles for recognition.

West Indies people still recall having live pain and the Wind Rush business makes it harder to take, for some managed to come over and made children here in England and even brought over their family from the islands, but all of a sudden, they are being rejected after years of toiling and building up this country. They have to fight again for a right to stay in this country after so many years of hard work. Some are even shamefully deported.

The Ark by TG

When God told Noah, build an ark
Did Noah ask, why
Did Noah ask, upon what shore
Should this great vessel lie

So God laid down the cubit size
And named the gopher wood
And pitch to hold that hulky rise
For God knows what is good

And when God brought the beasts of prey
Along with caring mate
Did any snarl and spoil the day
Or entering hesitate

This is obedient man and beast
That took God at his word
None wondered of the coming feast
All safe and sound on board

Outside the ark, the waters raged
Engulfing sin and shame
A fool, Almighty God assuaged
While earth rebuked his name

When at the end of the forty days
God brought the ark to a stand
He knew the old-world wicked ways
Had perished at his command.

Unscramble the ALPHABETADUKO words on the following pages

from the Unique Letters Below

1.   N U B L A M S R C E   10 letter Word

2 S   C   J   U   T   I   E   7 Letter Word

3 R   E   C   I   P   U   O   S   8 Letter Word

4 O   X   S   N   E   C   U   L   I   9 Letter Word

5 L   P   A   T   I   E   D   7 Letter Word

6 N   C   T   O   I   A   6 Letter Word

7   A   F   T   I   N   5 Letter Word

8   Y   N   I   T   U   5 Letter Word

9   S   I   H   R   E   V   6 Letter Word

10   R C A T S O I U P E N   11 letter word

Unscramble based on the clue given

1   C   L   S   D   R   E   M   A   B   9 Letter Word

Clue Not Revealed

2   M   L   E   R   A   S   6 Letter Word

clue Spirit Classes

4   L   A   P   E   C   I   S   7 Letter Word

clue Unique

5   N   O   T   U   C   I   E   R   A   P

10 letter word   clue Careful

6   G   O   B   I   T   A   E   L   D

     9 letter Word   clue An Oat

7 D   O   M   N   T   A   E   S   I   9 Letter Word

clue Control

8 H   U   R   I   S   O   N   7 Letter Word

clue Healthy

9 H   I   G   E   U   R   O   T   S   9 Letter Word

clue Justified

10   C   D   A   E   S   R

6 Letter Word   clue Precious

How many words can you find from each unscrambled set of letters? For Example out of N U B L A M S R C E, I will write a few words, continue finding more words. Do this for all the AlphaBetaDuko words above.

1. **Blame**
2. **Number**
3. **Scam**

How many words can you find from each unscrambled set of letters? For Example out of H I G U R T O E S, I will write a few words, continue finding more words. Do this for all the AlphaBetaDuko words above.

1. **Right**
2. **Sort**

How many words can you find from each unscrambled set of letters? For Example out of D I M A N T O E S, I will write a few words, continue finding more words. Do this for all the AlphaBetaDuko words above.

1. **Domain**
2. **Toes**

R	I	H	O	N	E	S	T	Y	Y	U	L	J
I	P	S	Z	O	N	F	T	P	F	E	A	J
G	S	R	E	T	A	I	L	P	I	X	I	A
H	I	A	E	I	N	E	A	R	N	C	D	X
T	P	E	N	C	A	R	E	F	U	L	E	T
E	R	T	E	E	A	R	E	F	U	L	L	U
O	E	L	E	C	L	U	I	A	T	S	B	P
U	C	H	C	M	E	U	T	E	A	I	M	O
S	I	N	S	I	P	I	N	I	R	O	A	S
O	O	S	I	I	G	P	E	I	O	N	R	I
U	U	N	P	U	R	I	G	H	T	N	C	N
L	S	A	E	E	R	U	P	E	O	Y	S	G
L	A	I	C	E	P	S	O	U	B	I	N	K
L	R	I	E	T	U	E	R	N	L	S	U	L
E	O	E	D	N	I	I	E	V	I	E	P	A
S	H	R	I	E	S	O	E	A	G	C	L	W
S	S	A	D	H	R	S	N	N	A	I	A	T
U	A	R	E	E	R	C	A	S	T	T	I	S
A	O	D	O	M	I	N	A	T	E	S	T	U
C	O	M	P	U	T	E	R	S	D	U	E	M
H	D	E	S	O	P	A	T	X	U	J	D	S
O	R	A	C	U	L	A	C	I	P	O	R	T
R	E	R	A	S	A	I	N	T	I	N	Y	I
E	A	E	R	N	I	O	T	S	E	C	N	A
S	M	A	E	A	T	S	H	R	I	V	E	L
T	S	E	D	I	S	H	R	I	V	E	N	P

son	fatigue
sins	computers
sun	precaution
tea	precious
ruin	scrambled
soul	unscrambled
area	justice
Lord	exclusion
side	obligated
near	righteous
tiny	honesty
unify	notice
unity	dominates
faint	acne
actions	plaiters
special	tropical
careful	must walk
nourish	laid
sacred	pepsi
scared	right
shrivel	chores
shriven	saint
plaits	cord
dreams	tears
realms	juxtaposed
sing	nourished

Dear Lord

Please speak to me

In words that make so clear

Where everything you offer

To the world I need to hear

Hold me upright in thy hand

And teach me more of love

So I can reach at thy command

And make thy message clear.

A BIT OF DUST

A bit of dust, that's what I am
Yet God found time for me
Created in his image, I am
He breathed his breath in me

And now I promise him endlessly
Whatever the day brings forth
My watchword then is "Christ for me"
Throughout the blessed earth

So let the God of heaven reign
In my contended heart
His Son doth take away my stain
And in him, set me part

By Thomas J Gage (TG)

Love, In Other Words Charity

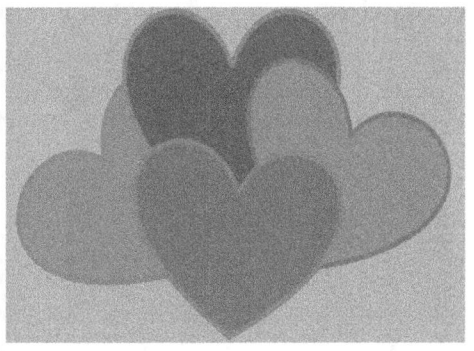

Love knows no boundary, just honesty,
God himself operates in love, in other
words charity,
Love is continual, not partial, not
circumstantial,
Sin on the other hand, a habit of it, is
daringly perpetual,
Sometimes love can be a right challenge,
True love a sacrifice never out of vantage,
So be just, be positive, not, high minded,
Not provoking, not lying, but be constructively guided,
Patiently pause to calculate your every responses,
Have non-submissions to evil advances,
Don't go around hating your brother,
You'll be then called a murderer,
Grow in love, let no evil penetrate,
Ward off the evil sufferings and pain as you supplicate,
Praying that insensitivity, unappreciative brutish behaviour, obliterate,
While consciously wholeheartedly seek to communicate.

Good Love shows up when you seek to be genuine,
So let the joys of love automatically kick-in,
Grab there principles to manufacture in you good Love,
Agape love, storge love, philos love, eros love,
Demonstrations of love sometimes make you look weak,
Let your attitude, actions, motives speak, just be meek,
When God love, family love, friendship love, romantic love, strong,
Anger, falsehood, furiousity gone, hands made strong all day long,
Your heart feels another's pain, travailing for gain,
Your brain triggers right than wrong, again and again,
It won't be a chore to lend a helping hand,
You'll be motivated even without someone's command,
No opportunity to say, 'once bitten twice shy',
Your discerning heart hears the cry and will not deny,
Your brain switch on flowing words tapered in love,
Shows a heart who knows good value
and the greatest which is Love.

By

Margaret Alicia Gage-Forrester

Love covers a multitude of sins. 1 Peter 4 18

Perfect love cast out fear for fear is torment 1 John 4:18
The Greatest commandment is TO LOVE,
when we love, we take on God's character and is able to do things like He does.
The greatest commandment would not be a chore for that will become our
nature as we take on Christlikeness

And thou shall love the Lord thy God with all thy heart,
all thy mind and all thy soul and all thy strength,
and Love thy neighbour as thy self.

The greatest commandment is to LOVE
To Love God,
To Love Self,
To Love your neighbour

John 3: 16 Tells us that God so loves us (whosoever) that if we believe in him
we will not perish but have everlasting life.

Perfect love cast out fear for fear is torment 1 John 4 18

Love is a fruit of the spirit and a gift of the spirit without Love we are nothing.
1 Corinthians 13:3 says, And though I bestow all my goods to feed the poor,
and though I give my body to be burned, and have not charity (love), it
profited me nothing.

Montserrat, 1980

Island of my birth,
Fresh sweet air,
People of great mirth,
Tiny, yet big of heart and fair.

Sparkling like the gem that gave it name,
The Emerald Isle lay shining in the sea,
Its beauty putting other isles to shame,
With awe indwell in its ecstacy.

A sea so blue beneath the paler sky,
And Mountain peaks that's rich in vegetation.
The breezer laugh or mourn, sometimes they sigh,
My! write me a poem! a recitation!

Perhaps old Neptune on that long gone day,
Let fall this jewel as he passed that way,
And so forgetting to retrieve once more,
Left it lying on the sandy shore.

By
My grandfather
Thomas Joseph Gage, 1980

All Those Of You Who Like To Interfere

Satan have room for schemers,
When you come through the window and not the door,
You are a thief and a robber, there is a door.
You enter in without permission, even if you obtain a key,
As long as it is without the owners' permission,
You're still a thief and a robber.

When you interfere with people's property and you know it is not yours,
It is not just covetousness, you are practicing to steal,
Sooner or later the path set for people like these,
Will be yours without fail.
What path this is, sure no place temperate,
Why don't you do things right for once in your life,
You can fool me but you can't fool God who watches constantly,

And before you get the better of me I am done
To all those of you who like to interfere,
before you get the better of me I am done!

By
Margaret Alicia Gage-Forrester

The Map Seat

They look at us like they're looking past us
We are asked to pardon or excuse
We stare back at them just as hard as they peer through us until we finally understand
The tourists need to see the map
They don't know where they're going

And tonight I'm in the map seat
So they look at me
They look through me
They've come from a distant continent
called Everyplace Else
And they plan to enjoy their visit,
 I can't relate
I come from the same place as the map
I'm a creature of the map itself
These colors are my colors
And the colors of my friends

"SAY MATE, is this train going North or South?"
"We are on now, the express, yes?"
"Pardon me bruh. I don't mean to bother you
 or nothing like that but umm..."
They do bother me, But I help anyway
I hope they enjoy their time here
I wish them a safe trip
I lean my head against the map and close my eyes
Until High Street at least, if not farther.
I'm a creature of the map itself...

By
Zachary Kenrick (Zach Mimble) Cabey

My Brother

Dust In My Face

Don't throw no dust in my Face,
We are supposed to be going the same place,
With one aim and ambition,
Travelling the narrow road in one direction,
So if you see me dragging my feet,
Remind me it's the Saviour I'm trying to meet,
Whenever I bend over, gently pick me up,
Don't let my stomach erupt,
Stretch forth your hand so I can recover,
Instead of watching me twisted and bent over,
Don't let me go blind,
Water, feed, awake my mind,
As you know this race is a process,
To progress one must continually confess,
So don't purposely push me behind,
Train me to renew my mind,
Hold my hands, nudge me forward in this race,
Instead of throwing dust in my face.

Why hit me and throw me off track,
Don't you know the lamp upon my feet will lead me back,
I neither want to see you go back,
Be trapped, get hacked, nor go off track,
You don't want to be told, 'go back and find,
Those confused delusional people you left behind!'
Twill be difficult thing to manuvre and push on,
You'll get crushed and trampled upon.
Think about it, the road is narrow,
The force of the people coming forward will hit you like an arrow,
Those people confused, bumping into walls unintentional,
They're blinded, can't see, dust in their eyes,
For the many times you raised the dust, unrecognize,
And the mere sight of this will make you delusional.
So let's grasp fast a new perspective, a new paradigm,
Running prepared steadfastly towards the finish line,
Let me remind you, we are sinners saved only by grace,
And it is through Jesus Christ alone our sins are erase,
So don't deliberately throw dust in anybody's face,
We are still trying to get to the same place.
Heaven bound, Jesus crown.

By **Margaret Alicia (Farrell) (Cabey) Gage-Forrester**

This is a poem that was birth out of a vision or dream that I saw. It was hard to carry as I prayed it through. It was pertaining to leadership.

For you don't want to be told go back and find, those confused delusional people you left behind. This speaks of a picture of someone running on in the race pushing over people as they go along but when they got to the master in all that speed they were told to go back and find the confused delusional people they left behind. May we fix all the things we need to fix on our journey and may we not make people confused for it is possible that when we think we are safe that the master would let you know that you have left people confused and that you need to go back and rescue them. When I saw the person going back the image of them being trampled upon was apparent. The thought that the person may not make it back is also apparent, so, please don't go running swiftly forward without fixing things that went wrong with people for you may not make it back if you have to go back and find. Learn to walk in forgiveness for you don't know how and when your journey will end.

If you confess your sins he is faithful and just to forgive you of your sins and cleanse you from all unrighteousness. 1 John 1:19

The Storm Is Gone

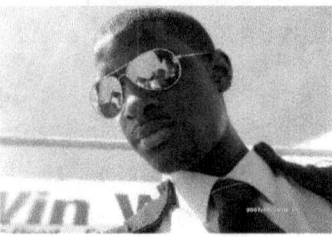

By Jordain Johnson, at 10 years old

The wind howls, ramps and rages,
The kettle screams and steams,
The lamppost stands there like a statue,
While the trees are pointing at you,
The grass shivers and swims in the wind,
My Television (TV) coughs and crackles,
All the clouds seem to cry, sigh,
As the lightening lights up the sky,
The sun is long gone,
And the moon cannot be seen,
The sky begins to go purple-green,
Suddenly, the sun comes out, It fights the clouds,
The place seems a bit light,
The sky is bright,
The storm is gone!
The clouds are gone,
The rainbow makes a bridge across the sky,
It is calm! I can see the sky,
The clouds no longer sigh,
Up comes the sunrise,
Beautiful, radiant blue skies, undisguised.
The storm is gone!

Written by

Wilston Jordain (WJRJ) "OutlawTheArtist" Reuben Johnson at Essex Primary School, United Kingdom

Birthday Greetings From My Son

The World's Best Mother with love on Mother's Day

This Mother's Day message comes especially for you to Wish you a very special day. Fond thoughts of you are always vet much in mind and it's hoped today will bring happiness and treasured memories.

HAPPY MOTHER'S DAY Mum!

Jordain words in the card said...

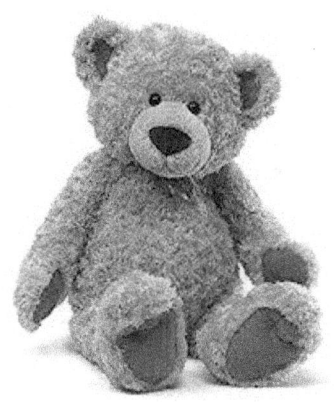

It's that special day called Mother's Day;

Wen I remember that you paid,

Virtually your own weight in gold;

To see me live another day,

I'm not the best son everyday,

But I've got to let you know;

I appreciate all your patience with my pace;

You will reap the benefits one day.

xxx

by my Son,

Wilston Jordain Reuben Johnson

He also gave me a stuff teddy bear for my Mother's Day and I kept it all the years. I lost it when I was evicted from my apartment in Manor Park. It made me sad.

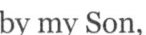

May 23, 2015

Eccentric woman

As the first to be born to our mother,
You are a gift and a blessing from the very start.
You carry a wealth of incomparable knowledge,
artful beauty, and inner strength.
Throughout your life, you've accomplished so much
Although given so little and stripped of so much.
You've reared a very respectable, Wonderful young man on your own,
And given your heart and time to so many others for God's glory.
I pray today that everyone entering your life from this day forward will
realize the exceptional spirit within the eccentric woman
And that they are all heightened in their talents
And generosity for your sake and benefit (to the glory of God, Amen!).

Big sister,
I love you.
Happy Birthday.

From my little sister Christelle N. Cabey

Sin Must Be Atoned

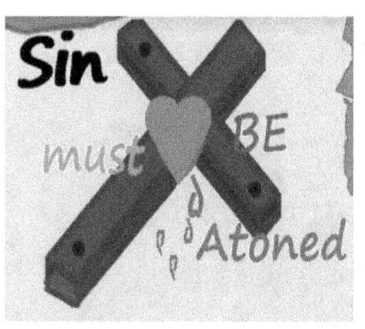

Sin must be atoned ...
After Satan interrupted, was it ever atoned?
We messed up the perfect design,
We circummed to Satan cohearsing the mind,
We ate of the good and evil tree, the forbidden,
We allowed Satan to disturb, that painless journey we had in Eden,
Now only one important tree left, it's embedded with eternity,
That's the tree of Life, access to God's infinity,
Quick! A love gesture from God's thoughtful heart,
Angels, bar the gate! Provisions needed from damnation's aught,
Atonement first please! Recompense! Sin not here with me!
Naked and knowledgeable as you have become now, please believe me,
See the angels barring the gate, it is FOR YOUR SAKE
So, don't you dare put forth your hand ON THAT TREE ABD TAKE.

So on you go, feel the consequence of your reaction,
Adam toil, till the soil, acquire to your heart's satisfaction,
Eve multiply, yes Eve, multiply, but not without pangs,
You see, earth does need you, but on you, childbirth pain hangs,
I never intended Satan tricks to meddle with my earth's dominion,
I merely took a rib from Adam, to make his companion,
You guys should have stuck with me and be content,
Now, unless you repent and accept my Son's atonement,
Sin in you permeates, the promise of eternity, a distant dream,
See, His body was nailed, pierced, crown dug deep, the agony still scream,
Can you hear it, the job was done, it was completely finished,
Yet man still sealed the tomb, but his significance was never diminished,
Redemptive authority given, keys taken, Christ emerged STRONG,
Resurrected triumphantly, with all power, to deliver our WRONG.

So was sin ever atoned? Yes, it was atoned,
Through Christ Jesus, the Son, sin was atoned,
But unless you accept His exchange of atonement,
Your dream of eternity will only ever mean torment,
Sin in you will generate, heaviness and discontentment,
No peace, no love, just more and more resentment,
No true joys, just temporary façade,
While your heart of sorrow is perpetually enlarged,

Even the mere site of you, sometimes, make other people nauseous,
And if it wasn't for the blood of Jesus, they'll be knocked unconscious,
So don't resist, surrender! Accept the offer with which, the blood defends,
So your sinful heart, can, in righteousness, live, and be cleanse,
On that painful journey through Calvary, Christ already, made AMENDS,
(And if you grasp that value)
And if THE TRUTH is allowed to illuminate in you, you'll be singing,
HALLELUJAHs, AMENs
For sin was atoned.

by

Margaret Alicia Gage-Forrester August 28th, September 9th & September 19th, 2012

We must accept his exchange of forgiveness of sin in order to enter into the paradise where Jesus says he is gone to prepare for us, or else we'll never be content, we will never make it when he returns to get his people according to John 14. He has gone to prepare a place for us and he is coming again to receive us unto himself that where he is there will may be also.

This poem was a journey for me. I could have only recorded it as a poem to get the audience to relate and I hope you do, for it was a powerful Holy Ghost moment in my life. It was as if I was arrested to do this one. It ran over three days. I could have heard some of the words in an audible voice.

I wanted to stop at stanza one but I couldn't. Another day came and more words just kept flowing. Resurrected triumphantly with all power to deliver our wrong, wow! Stanza three came on another day as a confirmed answer to the question, was sin ever atoned? Affirmatively, YES! through Christ Jesus the son, sin was atoned.

This poem has many bible scriptures to back up the meaning of it and I could never exhaust choices of scriptures to support for there are so many from Genesis where sin began to the New Testament.

Wherefore, as by one man (Adam) sin entered into the world, and death by sin; and so death passed upon all men, for that all have sinned: Romans 5:12

..Behold the man is become as one of us, to know good and evil, and now, lest he put forth his hand and take also of the tree of life and eat and live for ever. .... The Lord God sent him forth from the garden... Genesis 3:22-23

by the offence of one (Adam) judgment came upon all men to condemnation; ... by the righteousness of one (Jesus) the free gift came upon all men unto justification of life. Romans 5: 18

..by one man's disobedience many were made sinners, ... by the obedience of one shall many be made righteous. Romans 5:19

For all have sinned and come short of the glory of God Romans 3:23

For the wages of sin is death, but the gift of God is eternal life through Christ Jesus our Lord. Romans 6:23

.. by one man, Jesus Christ, hath abounded unto many. Romans 5:15 For if by one man's offence death reigned by one; much more they which receive abundance of grace and of the gift of righteousness shall reign in life by one, Jesus Christ. Romans 5:17

If my people which are called by my name shall humble themselves and pray, seek my face, and turn from their wicked ways, then, will I hear from heaven, and forgive their sins and heal their land. II Chronicles 7:14

For whosoever shall call upon the name of the Lord shall be saved. Romans 10:13

If we confess our sins, he is faithful and just to forgive us our sins, and to cleanse us from all unrighteousness ... 1 John 1:19

For God so loved the World he gave his only begotten son that whosoever believeth in him will not perish but have eternal life. John 3:16

..God commendeth his love toward us, in that, while we were yet sinners, Christ died for us. Romans 5:8

.. But we also joy in God through our Lord Jesus Christ, by whom we have now received the atonement. Romans 5:11

Whosoever therefore resisteth the power, resisteth the ordinance of God: and they that resist shall receive to themselves damnation. Romans 13:2

..As sin hath reigned unto death, even so might grace reign through righteousness unto eternal life by Jesus Christ our Lord. Romans 5:21

As I live, saith the Lord, every knee shall bow to me, and every tongue shall confess to God. Romans 14:11

My lips shall greatly rejoice when I sing unto thee and my soul which thou has redeemed. Psalm 71:23

I hope this poem is an eye opener and a blessing to the reader for I went on a journey when I wrote this one.

Empty But Not For Long!

The floor is empty, I confess to you,
The floor is empty But it won't be for Long,
Bubble up, bubble up, Oil bubble up,
The level is rising, bubble up,
It won't be for Long
Make space for the over flow,
Dig your ditches still while you tarry,
Overflow spill over to our children,
Our husband, our sisters and our brothers,
Our neighbours,
No waste, no waste.
Empty but Not For Long,
Not For Long, not For Long,
I confess to you the floor-room is empty,
But Not For Long, not for long!
Bubble up, bubble up, oil bubble up!

By
Margaret Alicia Gage-Forrester

Isaiah 60:18 wasting nor destruction within thy borders.
John 6:12 Nothing lost, nothing wasted.

The Floor Is Empty

Although the threshing floor is empty and is in need of grapes to press in order to get wine, the time comes when there will be an overflow of blessing.

Yes an overflow that should not be wasted. John 6:12-13 When they were filled, he said unto his disciples, Gather up the fragments that remain, that nothing be lost. Therefore they gathered them together, and filled twelve baskets with the fragments of the five barley loaves, which remained over and above unto them that had eaten.

The day will come when there is an overflow. Won't always be down and empty. Empty but not for long. Empty but Not for long.

Lord my storage is empty and I am available to you. I will not be defeated. I will not be denied. I will press till my overflow comes. Empty but not for long!

Liberate Yourself My Child

Liberate yourself my Child,
I know you've been struggling for a long while,
But your sins are forgiven, barriers broken down,
Rise, look, sing! Your victory has come,
Shake the dust off your feet and dance,
Pickup your boots and advance,

Do you know who you are?
Now is the perfect time to discover,
Don't you go under, pursue your saviour,
Forget the oppressor, you've got divine favour,
So march on my brother, press on my sister,
This is your hour, this is your moment of honour.

Are you baffled? Are you surprise?
Don't try to understand, just rise!
I know, doors shutting, doors opening, don't wonder,
The cattle on a thousand hills belongs to your Master.
So let go the old, grasp the new!
Who me? Yes you! The Master is calling you.

Bring your talents, your gifts, bring your trowels,
Chosen and beloved of God, it is time to dig wells,
So reach out my brother, step out my sister,
This is your hour, this is your moment of honour.

Written by

Margaret Alicia Gage-Forrester

Reformed Character

Sometimes I lose my strength, (I lose my strength)
When they tie me down, (when they tie me down)
But I am going to get it back, (I will get it back)
When I get it back I'm gonna pounce again,
(I will pounce again, I will pounce again)
It's restoration time, restoration come,
I will sing for joy, I will sing for joy,
Hallelujah, restoration ti me, restoration come, restoration come

Sometimes I lose my strength,
I lose my strength, when they tie me down,
When they tie me down,
But I am going to get it back,
I will get it back.
When I get it back I'm gonna pounce again.
I will pounce again.
It's restoration time, **restoration** come,
Restoration come, Hallelujah! Hallelujah!
Hallelujah, restoration come, restoration come,
I will get it back, I will get it back,
I'm gonna get it back, Hallelujah! Hallelujah!

By Margaret Alicia (Farrell) (Cabey) Gage-Forrester

This is a song

Definition for POUNCE
What is pounce: to jump or move quickly in order to catch or take hold of
something pursuing with vigour and determination. synonyms: leap,
spring, jump, swoop, dive, lunge.

GOD MADE

God made the moon a beauty of the night

He made the sun a blessing for the day

The stars of countless entity delight

The world by their magnificence warm the day

Should the cloud appear by misty thought

All nature gathers round in deep concern

Just vapour paying homage at its ought

A heavenly tribute given in sweet return

So nature works, so it was meant to be

Till some external inferior pride

Rose from it fair of immortality

Now confronted nowhere left to hide

Must face the consequence which summoned forth Calvary

By Thomas J Gage (TG)

Supposing I

Supposing I could never write or read
The wonderful things the Lord hath said to me
So I may understand and in my heart concede
That he is God through all eternity

Supposing I had put my trust in man
Who eats and sleeps and in the end doth die
Who doth nought unless God says he can
Confound, confound thee every lie

I thank you Lord through this simplicity
I may show someone searching for thy word
That just a lifted life in prayer can be
The reading of that line to find the Lord

Lord let me not rise a single morn
With thoughts not set on thee
Let me behold each rising dawn
In prayer on bending knee

By Thomas J Gage (TG)

Young Black People – Dichotomise

By Jordain "OutlawTheArtist" Johnson 13 years old

Listen, I wanna say one thing out loud,
I know it's been used but, 'I'm black and I am proud',
Some would say on this celebration only negros allowed,
But nah, that would be a joke, Look, others in the crowd,
They would never miss out on why we say it so loud,
Why we walk with our heads held high above the clouds,
But wait! Let me exclaim our freedom with better words,
I'm sure my ancestors would smile if they heard,
'Ah u look pan ahwee picnee dem speakin big words',
Yeah that's what they would say if they knew where we were living,
Breathing, eating, sleeping, getting an education and some even
educating.
Back in the day, talk 'bout further education 'huh', Seven Standard,
Secondary School, Technical College, University - No way!
So we should use the education we can get today,
I remember my grandmother always use to say something about the
system being, 'Connivance, conspiracy, meddling with the laws of gain to
drown blackman,
There were many black faces in consternation, Having to live with a
consensus they didn't agree to,
Then finally the government knew what to do, And I hope you have too,
Cuz that was then and there is really nothing we can do,
Oh wait! sorry, there is something that we can do,
We can move onwards, upwards and forwards,
Growing and learning with no constraints,
Nothing holding us back, no more stabbing in the backs,
Come on, let's countermeasure this stigma that's been put on our backs.
Ha ha, bet u didn't know I knew words like that!

Ok, there's one other thing that I happened to notice,
Africans and Caribbeans, Awarakians and Caribs seem to dichotomise,
Listen, we should be helping each other to rise,
Not being a hindrance in a blacked out disguise,

But I don't really want to gesticulate all this verbal diarrhoea,
Just trying to emphasize the fact that we should be sticking together,
Through rain, sleet, snow, volcano, hurricane and any weather,
Instead of our relationships being as thin as a feather,
So any little thing, it keeps us from been together,
Anyway, I know some of you are finding this boring,
So I'm done, I won't keep you snoring,
But there was one more thing I wanted to say here, I quote this from
Martin Luther King Jr, It's so important nowadays.
It's just a simple phrase, 'Can't we all get along!'
By Jordain Johnson

This poem was written in 30 minutes for black history month when my son was in Secondary School at the age of 13 years old. It was articulated by himself at a school youth concert in East London.

It proves that black people discriminate against themselves from one nation to another and this should not be. My son says 'can't we all get along'.

I am GRATEFUL!

Thank you God, Amen!

I might have lived by myself from a young age but I was NOT alone. I had friends and family and most of all I got Jesus who was always on my side even though I didn't know him personally yet. Praise God!

Father, I thank you for these who you placed in my (our) pathway in the past and I thank you now for forward and upward trajectory in the name of Jesus, Amen! Hallelujah!

Thank you for your patience with my pace. Thank you Lord!

If you have not accepted Jesus Christ as your Lord and Saviour, please pray this simple prayer in faith before you leave the page.

Father, Jehovah, Yahweh, in the name of Jesus your son,

I want to love you, I accept you as Lord and Saviour of my life. Please forgive me of my wrongs and wash away all my sins in the name of Jesus. I know that salvation belongs the Lord who sits upon the throne and unto the lamb, he who was slain for my sins. Forgive my sins and help me to become more and more like you in Jesus name.

I want to be ready when you return for your people, Jesus. So keep me always loving you Lord, in your name I pray.

Thank you for your love, Lord. Help me to love you back always and to walk in the right way in the name of Jesus, through the aid of your only presence here on earth, The Holy Spirit living within me.

Amen!

Hallelujah!

0	1	2	3	4	5	6	7	8	9
1									
2									
3									
4									
5			*L*						
6									
7									
8									
9									

created by: © M A G-F 2004

USE THESE LETTERS TO SOLVE THE ALPHABETADUKO PUZZLE

M L I F A N Y O E

UNSCRAMBLE In the space below 2 Words

							L	

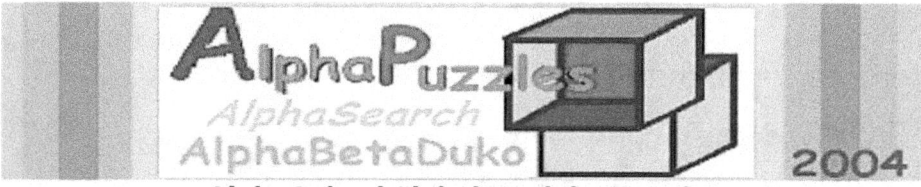

AlphaCube / Alphabetaduko Puzzles
How it works

0	1	2	3	4	5	6	7	8	9	
1										
2										
3										
4										
5			$\mathcal{L}$							
6										
7										
8										
9										

created by: © M A G-F 2004

AlphabetaDuko works as a mind exercise with 9 letters.

1. These 9 letters complete the 81 grid space Alphabetaduko puzzle. an example of the nine letters is below..

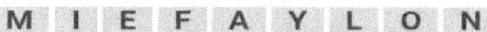

M I E F A Y L O N

- There can be absolutely no repeats in any of the columns or the rows.

2. - There is a 9 letter space grid with colour variation, within

that 9 letter space you will get the 9 letters without any repeat.

* so it is the rows, columns and the 9 space grid a 3X3 area.

example of 3X3 grid

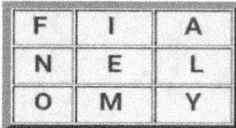

F	I	A
N	E	L
O	M	Y

3. - Then the 9 letters are used to solve an unscramble word or phrase. The indication/clue will be given further indication as to how many words to unscramble. Another clue, if the answer is a phrase, the spacing between the squares will tell you how many letters in each word of the phrase

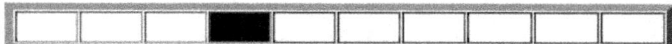

There are 3 spaces then blank then 6 spaces, so it is a TWO word phrase. The first word has 3

The Tempest Rage

The tempest rage, didn't he,

The wall stood stubbornly before me,

I'm imagining things, this just can't be

For the Holy one said, there is an open door before me,

So what, what is your ambition Mr Mountain,

No territory here for you to regain,

You spilt long years of stormy rain,

So give up now, O tempest, my vow I will maintain.

Clutched in my arms is that fulfilling thought,

That sufficiency is found in the Thou Art,

I will cleave to His promises never to depart,

Knowing that He will unfold like a majestic piece of art.

By

Margaret Alicia Gage-Forrester

Let Reuben Live

Jesus is love, that much I know,
I am thankful that he cares for us so,
Unconditional love is flowing,
Thank you Jesus, the all knowing,
Lord help my bloodline to serve you,
Turn back the stone that intended to pronounce Reuben death.
Let him know, it is Not Time Yet!
Bring life and breathe substance to his being,
Lord let Reuben live
To the glory of God in your name Jesus let him live
Amen!

By
Margaret Alicia Cabey Gage-Forrester

Feel for Me

If you was in the same predicament as I,
Seeing the same things when you open up your eyes,
The lose women being open with their guys,
And politician been open with their lies,
Cops firing shots, call it coping with the crime,
They declare a war on drugs, why does doping not decline?
Kids getting exit to the line where their innocence is gone,
They see picture on the screen that get frozen in their minds,
Now they boasting to the dimes how they holstering they nines,
Things would have been fine if their role model were moms,
This might have stopped if their role models were paps,
But they paps always gone and their momma run the block,
Not a role model that they got,
Shout about how often they got shot,
Or how they sold that potta for that drop,
How could you'll not, feel for me,
Or feeling the way I'm feeling for families with children,
Fighting for survival on the fringes, survival of the fittest,
For real its getting vicious, No more fighting with their fist its,
Just a flick of their finger and they'll be firing their biscuits,
Violence and mischief heightening the statistics,
Of black men dieing or in prison,
This is in my vision in the place where I'm living,
Feel for me, I will feel for you.

If you had your own paliful to deal with,
That felt damn near impossible to deal with,
And it is damn near palpable to feel it,
Make .... Platitude to seal it
Let it be known you are never alone,
When you get in that zone just listen to these poems,
There'll help you along when everything get hard,
Just help me along to ..... these songs,
Keep sending email I will respond,
Keep saying darg that song was hard,
I'll take that love and store it in my heart,
And give it back to you'll when I record,
When I proform for all of you'll,
And I go hard and when you'll applaud,
And you'll let on just how strong you feel for me,
Is like no other feeling that I did feel,

Is like no other feeling was ever as real,
So how the fans feel is a very big deal,
Try to satisfy you like a very big meal,
Always went hard and I never did chill,
Trying real hard just to better these skills,
And one of my award for my efferent skills you,
Feel for me and I will feel for you.

Joseph (ScribeTheVerbalist) Javayne Cabey
My brother

He is a lyricist, poet, rapper like my son. My son gets inspiration
from him at times.

Letters used in AlphaCube

Top grid

	0	1	2	3	4	5	6	7	8	9
1	S		R			S	D	N	I	
2			F	U	D					
3	N	H			R			F	U	
4	U	S	H		I	E	N	D		
5	F			H						R
6		R	I	N				S		
7	I	D			U			R	N	
8			S					U	H	
9			U	D		R	E			

Letters used in AlphaCube

D   S   H   F   R   E   N   I   U

Unscramble letters to form a word

Bottom grid

	0	1	2	3	4	5	6	7	8	9
1	H	S		I						U
2			F	H	S	U	R			
3	I	U	D	R				S	N	
4	E		U		H	R	D	I		
5		I	H	U	E			F	R	
6	R	F	S	D	I	N			E	
7	F			S	U	H	I		D	
8	S	D	I	N	R	F	E	U	H	
9	U	H	N	E			S	R		

R T E G I H O S U

Unscramble letters to form a word

	0	1	2	3	4	5	6	7	8	9
1	G	S		O						U
2			T	G	S	U	R			
3	O	U	H	R				S	I	
4	E		U		G	R	H	O		
5		O	G	U	E			T	R	
6	R	T	S	H	O	I			E	
7	T			S	U	G	O		H	
8	S	H	O	I	R	T	E	U	G	
9	U	G	I	E			S	R		

	0	1	2	3	4	5	6	7	8	9
1			S			G	T	I		
2	G	R	U	O	T					
3	I	H			S					O
4		G	H		R	E	I	T		
5	U			H						S
6		S	R	I				G		
7	R	T			O	H		S	I	
8			G				O	H		
9		U	O			S	E			

0	1	2	3	4	5	6	7	8	9
	L		T						A
F				E	A	T	L		
	A		F				Y	E	
		E		F			D		
L	F				T		E		
	T			L	I	A			
T	D			A					
		Y	I	D			T	L	
	E	L			N		A		

Letters used in AlphaCube

F N I L D E A T Y

Unscramble letters to form a word

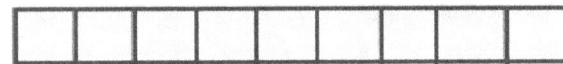

0	1	2	3	4	5	6	7	8	9
L	E	I			Y	D	N	A	
		F	E	D	N				
N	T			I			F	E	
	Y	T		A	L	N	D		
F			T						I
	I	A	N			T	Y		
A	D			E			I	N	
		Y				E	T		
		E	D		I	L			

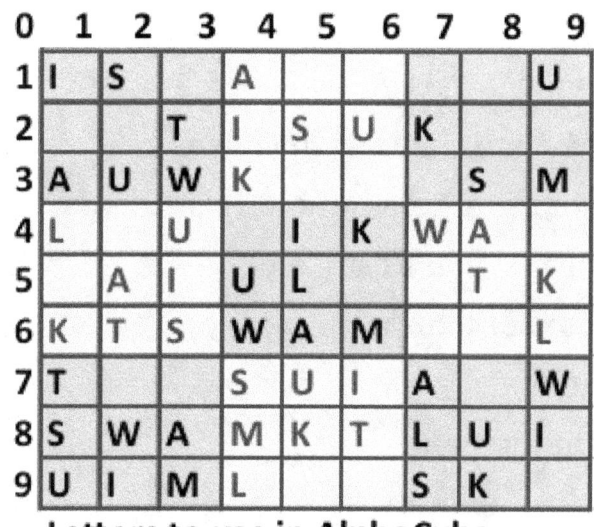

0	1	2	3	4	5	6	7	8	9
1 I	S		A						U
2		T	I	S	U	K			
3 A	U	W	K				S	M	
4 L		U		I	K	W	A		
5		A	I	U	L			T	K
6 K	T	S	W	A	M			L	
7 T			S	U	I	A		W	
8 S	W	A	M	K	T	L	U	I	
9 U	I	M	L			S	K		

Letters to use in AlphaCube

K A I M T U W S L

unscramble letter to form words

0	1	2	3	4	5	6	7	8	9
1 S		A			S	K	U	I	
2		M	L	K					
3 U	T			A			M	L	
4 L	S	T		I	W	U	K		
5 M			T					A	
6		A	I	U			S		
7 I	K			L			A	U	
8		S				L	T		
9		L	K		A	W			

Those Hands

Those hands hidden inside your jacket

Use them for right and they'll put money in your pocket,

Reflect on the attention your mothers put on those hands,

A good review bound to propel you to advance,

Those hands were made for something special

Don't sit there and be in denial

Take up the pencil, take up the pen

Ask for the slate, ask for the paper, then

Sit down and use them

Those hands, envision those hands

How many times before, you heard commands

Your hands are connected to your brain, your eyes, your ear

Portray what you understand, see and hear and don't shed a tear.

by

Margaret Alicia Gage-Forrester

Dedication to the Authenticated Geniuses Thomas Joseph Gage (TG) and Mary Sonia Gage Cabey and John Henry Gage

My grandfather Thomas J (Lee) Gage birthday May 3rd and mine, Margaret Alicia Gage-Forrester is 20 days later May 23rd. We had our own little thing going on with that. He would send me little notes of poetry in his handmade envelopes special delivery by the postman with his sophisticated penmanship.

Grandfather Thomas J. Gage have passed on from this life but he will not be forgotten. A man of deep thoughts, a writer, an artist, a reporter, a scribe, a satisfactory cook/baker, photographer, etc. Grandfather Thomas J. Gage wrote several writings. He wrote a book entitled "If Either Side Knew" A beautifully written detective type romantic book. I wish I still had a copy. Can't find it anywhere, if you happen to have a copy inbox me, it means much to me.

Father of Sonia (Lee) Gage Farrell Cabey who departed this earth 21st September, 2003, named by grandson Jordain Johnson as Sonia 'Junia' at the age of 2 1/2 or 3 years.

Joseph Scribe Cabey in Seattle, WA, United States, Second son of Sonia Cabey says, Alicia Gage-Forrester, learned the same love of poetry from M Sonia Gage Lee Galloway Farrell Cabey aka Mom. I miss her. I was just talking to a stranger today about how surprised I was to hear her say that she supported me pursuing a career as a rapper. I was 15 or 16 and I wasn't allowed to play rap music in the house but, she was my first favorite rapper.

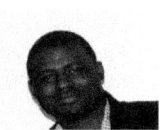

I used to love to hear her recite poetry and tell stories with those special intonations and animated gestures. Every character got her own funny voice and face.

M Alicia Gage-Forrester says, True! Artistic expression. Dramatic, she was not bland at all. Rapping is almost like spoken word/poetry. Scribe The Verbalist, she might have recognized that you have some of the same poetic ability as herself and that you are expressing it in a different way. You know mom was witty, you know that. That is also an art form ... you know how she wishes you to express art forms drawing, writing, and so, if rapping is one of them she would have embraced it. Therefore do good with it.

We Love them both! Mom and Grandfather.

Thomas J Gage was The first to put traffic signs on the roads in Plymouth town. Thomas J Gage, TG, man from Cherry Village, George Street, Central, Plymouth, Montserrat, BWI.

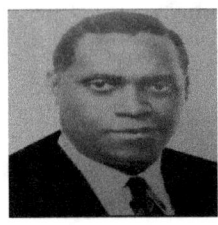

The young enterprising artist who they took out of school in Montserrat to make sketches of objects, products, items that were further copied and sent off for official use as a blue print including a carbon copy of problematic items to be fixed. He was a great artist. This is back in the day when we had no fax, no photocopiers, no modern-day computers to use.

Thomas J. Gage loved baking. He especially loved baking coconut tarts and pies just like his mothers, Alicia Lee and Moriah Trott. I looked forward to my pie wrapped in table cloth like the old story books pictures.

He has child, grandchildren and great-grandchildren who shows the same culinary artistic ability as well as drawings and paintings.

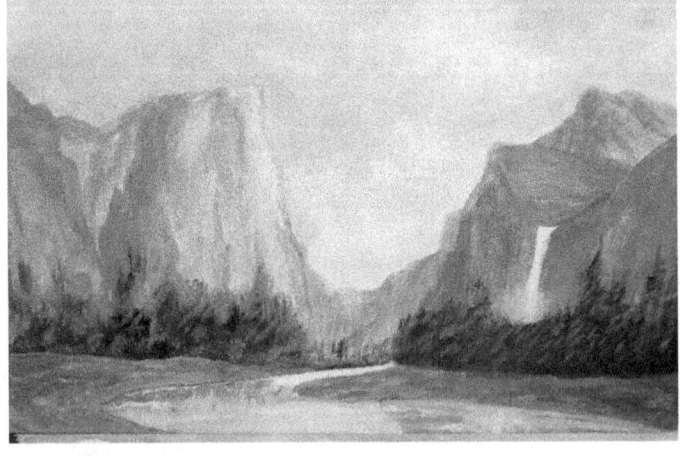

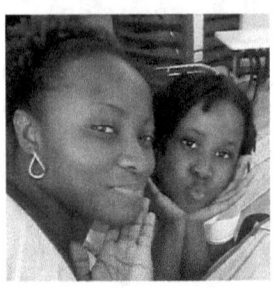

Art work by one of the grandchildren Christelle N. Cabey

Be it culinary art, Poetic art, Drawing and Painting, Literary art, Lyricism, anything arty. These are displayed in the grandchildren and great-grandchildren work.

Thank God for a strong gene from Thomas Joseph Gage. I pray for a strong blessing too in the name of Jesus.

Authentic!

Lord have mercy, he put his two hands on me at my mother's funeral. God bless his soul!

Being the oldest of the children it means allot as I carry such a burden for the souls of the others. May God equip me to endure in carrying the mantle correctly to His glory.

Chezline Riley second grandchild wrote:

With a heavy heart, I share the loss of my dear granddad, Thomas J Gage, author, poet, artist and illustrator, teacher and a devout Christian. He lived a great life but now the Master has seen fit to put him to rest.

Granddad, you lived your life with so much dignity and grace and passed on that legacy to your posterity, the ones now left to treasure and honor all that you were. Through your intelligence and passion for the arts, you've left behind a wealth of intellectual and artistic talents; artists, poets, singers, rappers, writers, painters, illustrators, and so much more. But most importantly, we all inherited your sense of dignity and big-hearted love for others. Your gentle and unassuming nature has been a balm to those who needed it and endeared you to so many. On behalf of my siblings, nephew and me, I bid you farewell. We love and will miss you, T J Gage. Sleep in peace.

GAGE, THOMAS JOSEPH.
If either side knew, by T. J. Gage.
New York, Carlton Press. 113 p.
(A Geneva book) © Thomas Joseph
Gage; 22May72; A342267.

"If either side knew"
A34·2267 May 22nd 1972

Your book, **"If Either Side Knew"** speaks volumes about your astute powers of perception and your great insight into this life you've traversed.

"If Either Side Knew" © Thomas Joseph Gage 1972 . New York. Carlton Press 113p 22nd May 1972 A34.2267.

Margaret Alicia Gage-Forrester also commented about another book **"When Satan Fell"**. Very Interesting personal analogy of what took place back there in the bible. It was written with deep engaging thoughts. *"When Satan Fell"* © Thomas Joseph Gage 2002

"Your father work with a will" is also a line from one of his poems. Thomas Gage is my grandfather and John H Gage, the mechanic engineer is my great grandfather, they both worked with a will. I quote the phrase all the time, "I work with a will". I don't short change or else I won't do it at all. I believe in an earnest days work which deserves an earnest days pay.

Chezline Riley said, That's right sis. It's how we do things. God will reward your diligence.

Thomas Joseph Gage was the son of the genius engineer, mechanic, musician, sailor, security guard. John Henry Gage of Montserrat, British West Indies.

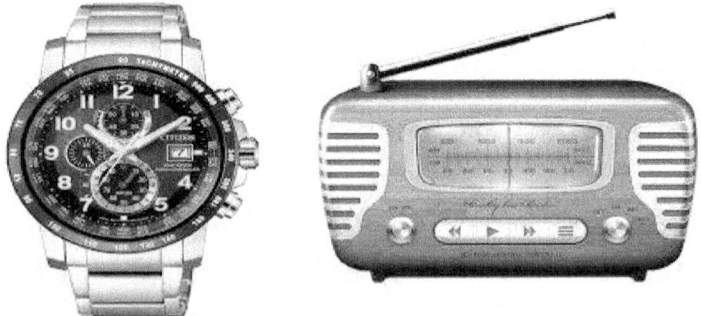

John Henry Gage, the genius engineer, musician. Cotton Jinery Mechanic and Jen Osbourne Trusted Employee. He secured the vault of Jen Osbourne business as security looked over. He fixed watches, radios, cars, boats and other machinery.

John Henry Gage loved music. He kept a velvet red Accordion in his room under his bed in the original casing until his death. He loved to play to me, Alicia. I took pleasure in going to his house at lunch time as he lived pretty close to the secondary school I went to. He would pull out his Accordion and play me a few tunes. I enjoyed this very much. My great grandfather made sorrel and ginger beer which he preserved for years. I would get a sip of the fermented drinks much to my delight. Great-grandfather was a devoted Christian right up to his death. It was a pleasure to spend time with him, I enjoyed every minute of it.

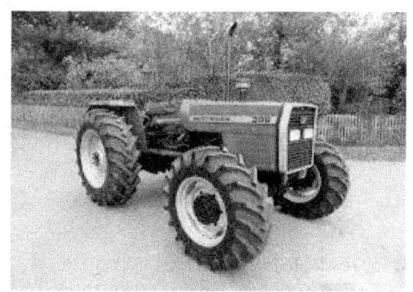 John Henry Gage is the First to put a mechanical vehicle together in Montserrat in Tar River, Long Ground, Eastern Corner in the early 1900s, in Plymouth, Montserrat, BWI and drove it to town. People who knew about it said it was a sight to see.

Thank you!

THANK GOD FOR THE MANY FAMILIES HE PUT ME IN, ALL of you God bless you and your children. I WAS RAISED AND I WAS SUPPORTED AND ACCEPTED BY COMMUNITIES OF PEOPLE AND I AM GRATEFUL.

I was supported and encouraged, loved and ministered to by Aunt Mae Daniel family from Parsons, Delores Placide family from Weekes, Esther Lynch Isaak family from Harris, Allen Family in St. Peters, Acka Family in Amersham, Nennen the grandmother of the Riley Family, Charlie Watts Maize family, Sis Eurit Family from Jamaica, lived in the Bronx and the entire Harvest Church Family under pastorship of Tom Grassano in the Bronx. The Edwards & Smith Family in Antigua, The Harrigan and Gumbs Family in Anguilla. My boss, Allen Stanford in Houston, the Montserrat and Antigua working family. The Dewar/Mageston Family, Joshua Francois and his friend Oral Coward and Family in Virginia. New Life Assembly Family in Dulwich and Dalston, England. The Westbury Baptist Church in Tottenham England. Magistrate Sister Anna Ryan of Trinidad and Sister Nurse Cooper of Bethany Church, Montserrat, we shared Ministerial love. My friends: Dorothymae Greenaway. Sheryle Meade and Daddy Simon. Denise Boston. Annie Daly Davis family from Olveston Salem and the Bronx.

Special thanks to Pickette Wilston Johnson, Jordain Johnson's dad for being my longterm friend and support. God bless you! Thank God you gave us a seed. Thank you Pickette for not spilling your bean, for not spilling it on the ground. In due season it produced fruit.

Jordain Johnson selected a frame, "God's Gift" for himself above Tigger, Winning The Poo and Donald Duck when he was a very young boy. Bless him

Father! Thank you for the light you gave him from a young age, continue on to shed light in and through him I pray in the name of Jesus. Father I ask that you bless him, Jordain Johnson, save him, cover him, protect him, shower him with blessings, lead him, inspire him and keep your hands on him on to eternity in Jesus name. Thank you for what you have already done and thank you in Advance for what you will do for him Father in Jesus name, Amen!

Thank God for my Parsons people in the name of Jesus. Just the best community of people to live around. Amen! Webbs was a great community too...in my grandmother, Mah Liz and Edwin world everything was super-duper.. Thank God for memories.

I thank God for the Catholic Church in Montserrat, God bless them. Father Mark and Father George in the name of Jesus. I especially thank God for Father Mark who allowed me to accompany them in ministry as they went out to minister to elderly and shut in people of the Montserrat community. I am also thankful to Sister Verna Brandt who asked me to come into the choir and showed the spirit of true hospitality. God bless them and shine his light upon them as they seek to forward their walk in the knowledge of God and his things to the return of his son Jesus Christ. Reveal your truths to them Father in the name of Jesus, Amen!

Thank God for Pastor Shane and Pastor Kellar of the Wesleyan Holiness Church in Montserrat who acknowledged my presence in their churches and especially for their words and prayer support. God bless them and their ministries. I thank you for Pastor Toney Allen of the Pentecostal Church and his prayer support and gifts while I was in Montserrat. God continue to bless him and open up himself to him in a new way to take the church forward in this season in the name of Jesus.

I thank God for Sister Hazel Riley and The Pastor of the Adventist Church in Montserrat who came to visit and encourage me while I was in hospital. Thank you for your prayers. God bless you both and expand your walk in him to the revealing of new truths for the advancement of knowledge to the people you serve for the preparedness of Jesus return in the name of Jesus.

I give high regard for the head of the Christian Council, Father V of the Anglican Church. I had a special bond to him as the head of the Christian body in Montserrat while I was there. I worshipped God and prayed for him as he came around the apartment complex to minister and I am thankful for his diligence in ministry. God bless him and strengthen him to lead the Church body aright in the name of Jesus!

Beverley Dewar was my encourager and friend and sister and mother when I was younger and extended family. Thank you Jesus for her. Bev loved Me and Jordain Johnson like her very own. She actually refer to us as her child, Daughter and grandchild, grandson. Nothing can change that. I will forever be grateful to God for Beverley Dewar. Praise God! Father bless her and her seed seed in the name of Jesus.

Thank God for Mrs Payne who walked around Montserrat from the Jehovah Witness Church telling people to Love God! Getting people to read and learn scriptures, and making sure every child had access to the orange-yellow bible story book to read. God bless her and her children in the name of Jesus...

All scriptures are given by the inspiration of God and is profitable for doctrine, for reproof, for correction, for instruction in righteousness, that the man of God may be PERFECT thoroughly furnished unto all good works. 2 Timothy 3 16-17 This scripture was planted in me since I was 7-8 years old and when it came to light in my soul and I recognize the power of it, I will always be thankful to God for Mrs. Payne from the Jehovah Witness Church. She had me and my sister learn the 2 verses, A corresponding scripture says more or less the same. Romans 15 4, Whatsoever things are written aforetime were written for our learning; that we through patience and comfort of the scriptures, might have hope.

Thank God for Brother Roper too. By the way they never forced me to read from a different bible, they told me bring my BIBLE and let's read and study together. I had a KJV Gideon red bible which my stepfather left in the house. I consider them true stalwarts of Discipleship Evangelism. God bless them and their children. The Bible says, Study to show thyself approved unto God a workman who does not need to be ashamed, rightly dividing the Words of Truth. 2 Timothy 2 15. 2 Timothy 3 15 says this, And that from a child thou hast known the holy scriptures, which are able to make thee wise unto salvation through faith which is in Christ Jesus. I always remind my son of this latter scripture.

I thank God for those who supported Jordain Johnson my son throughout his life... Aunt Mel, Randolph and family, auntie Jacquelyn and Screw, Terell Allen, auntie Debbie and uncle Eddie family, Diane Harrigan Gumbs and Javeed Ryan, Jeff Wilson, Sister Eurit and Michael, Sam and Alex and Pastor Thomas Grassano in the Bronx. Brother Wayne Greaves and Brother Danny. His Philippine family in Plaistow, England and the entire Eastlea School Family in Canning Town especially David Smith, Barbados born from the Youth Club. Pastor Conlon Carter of the Time Square Church in Manhattan New York, Saint Bons and Angeles Six Form College family in Forest Gate, England. Friends, teachers, families and associates in New York and California. I especially want to mention Jamal his friend and continual support. Thank God for the Boxhill family in Mount Vernon too. It is not easy living without your constant but you guys all made it much more manageable for him. Thank you very much. God bless you all!

Throughout my life I lived in Montserrat in several villages. I lived in Webbs Village, Plymouth Montserrat, Parson Village, Plymouth, Montserrat, LookOut Farrell Estate, Northern Corner, Montserrat, BWI. I also lived in Harris Village, Weekes Village, and in Saint Peters Parish, Montserrat, British West Indies. I lived in several places in New York city in America, in the Bronx, Queens and Brooklyn, after the volcano erupted and cut off the central to southern part of the island of Montserrat. Then, I moved to England in 2000 after my dad got sick. I lived in Milton Keynes, Stratford, Margate, Manor Park, Enfield, Tottenham, Edmonton, and now I live in Ponders End in England.

Life has been a journey for me but through the grace of God I am enduring.

Thanks to the many who supported Me, and My son Jordain Johnson. I also thank God for all those who supported my brother Earlson Daley-Farrell (Cabey) in Montserrat, the United States, Antigua and in England. Thank You! God return blessings unto you in the name of Jesus.

I might have lived by myself from a young age but I was NOT alone. I had friends and family and most of all I got Jesus who was always on my side protecting me. Praise God! I spent my time making games, writing and reading poetry and after I got saved, I engaged in prayer, Evangelistic Ministry outreach and reading of the word. I also volunteered in many places including Brixton Prison here in England.

GRATEFUL! Oh so grateful! Thank you, God. Father, I thank you for these who you placed in my (our) pathway in the past. Thank you for the readers. All their support is well appreciated.

I thank you now for forward and upward trajectory in the name of Jesus. Amen!

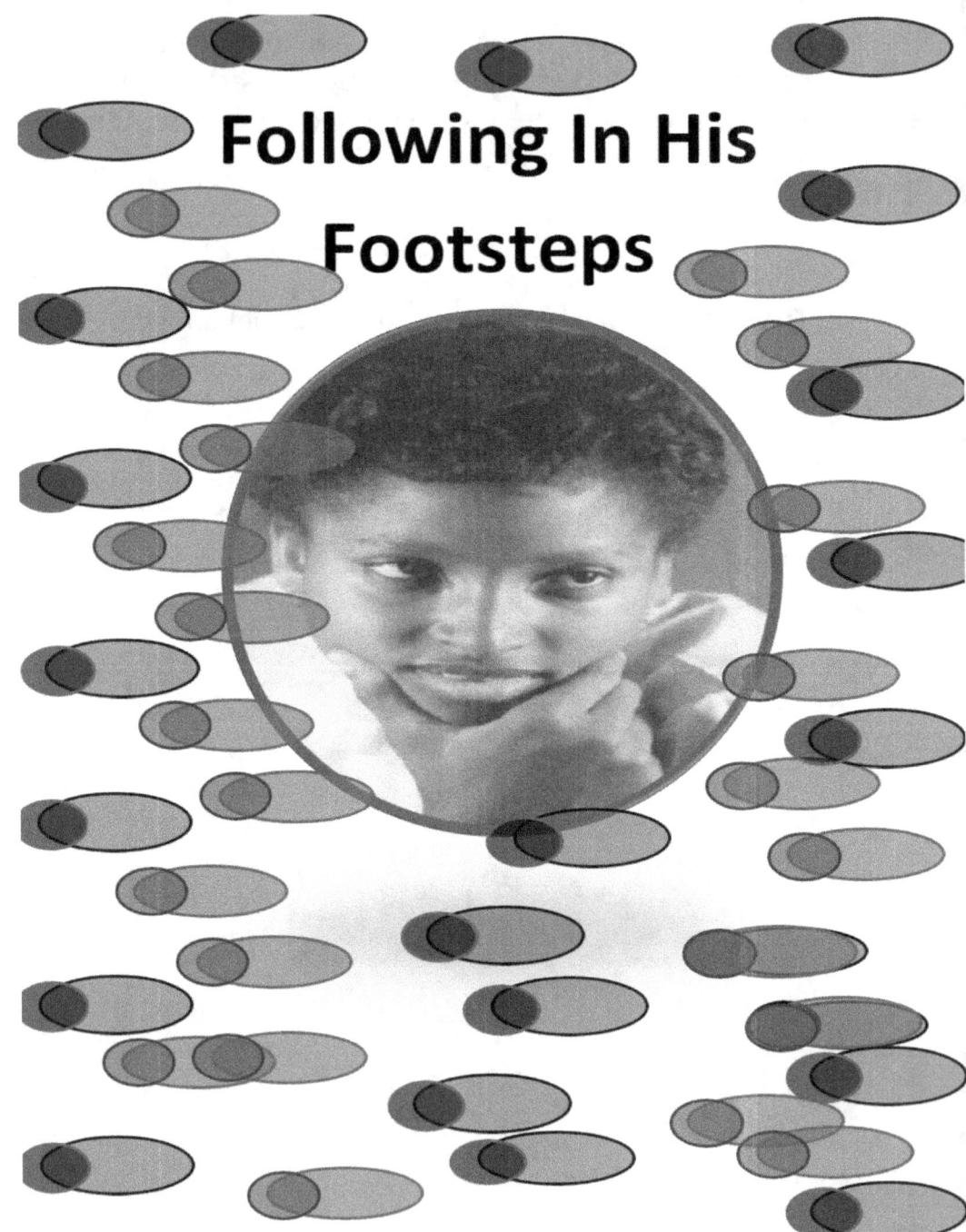

Following In His Footsteps